FAMILY FUN UNPLUGGED

Dedicated to my incredible loving parents, Emer and Art, and my very supportive eight siblings affectionately called: Ruaraldas, Lucretia, Clarissa, Jopus, Mavis, Ronaldo, Gino and Ellen Melon.

PETER COSGROVE

FAMILY FUN UNPLUGGED

MIND-BOGGLING RIDDLES, TRICKS, BRAIN-TEASERS AND LOADS MORE ACTIVITIES TO ENTERTAIN THE ENTIRE FAMILY

PENGUIN IRELAND

UK | USA | Canada | Ireland | Australia
India | New Zealand | South Africa

Penguin Ireland is part of the Penguin Random House group of companies
whose addresses can be found at global.penguinrandomhouse.com.

First published 2019

001

Copyright © Peter Cosgrove, 2019

The moral right of the author has been asserted

Typeset and designed by Kazoo Independent Publishing Services
Cover design by Andrew Brown
Illustrations by Padraig O'Connor

Printed and bound in Great Britain by Clays Ltd, Elcograf S.p.A.

A CIP catalogue record for this book is available from the British Library

ISBN: 978–1–844–88480–3

www.greenpenguin.co.uk

CONTENTS

CHAPTER 1

RIDDLES AND TEASERS

Whether you are a child or an adult you will find these to be some of the most challenging riddles. It is always nice to be the smartest person in the room! Challenge as many of your friends and family as you can!

ANIMALS

1. Name an animal that can jump higher than an elephant.

2. A chimpanzee is tied to a piece of rope that is 3 metres long. There is a bowl of grapes 10 metres away. How can the chimpanzee reach the bowl without cutting the rope?

3. This creature has 100 feet in the air yet its back is still on the ground. How is this possible?

4. If an elephant weighs 5 tons and you have a truck that can carry 49 tons, how many elephants can you fit into the empty truck?

5. Lara has a dog that is on the other side of a deep, wide river. There is no bridge and the only way to the other side is across the river. Yet the dog is able to cross the river without getting wet. How?

6. A dog gives birth to 3 little puppies - a brown one, a white one and a black one. What was the mother's name. You should know the answer from the information you've been given, so what was the mother's name?

7. There are 6 birds sitting in a tree. A hunter shoots 1 of them. How many birds are in the tree now?

8. Two cats - a fat one and a thin one - are sitting on the porch. The fat cat is the son of the thin cat, but the thin cat is not the father of the fat cat. How is this possible?

9. There are 30 cows in a field, 20 ate chickens. How many didn't? (This riddle is all about reading aloud, as '20 ate' sounds like '28', so your friend will keep asking you to repeat it as they won't understand.)

WORDS

1. What word has KST in the middle, in the beginning and at the end? This is a word you know and it is in the English dictionary.

2. What 5-letter word becomes shorter when you add 2 letters to it?

3. What 4-letter word (written in capitals) can be written forwards, backwards or upside down and can still be read from left to right?

4. A carnival worker told a boy: "If I can write your exact weight on this piece of paper you have to give me £100, but if I cannot I will pay you £100." There were no weighing scales nearby. The boy agreed. How did he lose the bet?

5. What 2 words have the most letters when combined?

6. What common English word describes a person or thing that cannot be found in or at any place, but when a single space is added also describes a person or thing that is present at this moment?

7. Which word does not belong in the following list? drop, crop, cop, lop, mop, shop or prop.

8. Let's test your grammar. Which is correct: "Tomatoes are a pretty vegetable" or "Tomatoes is a pretty vegetable"?

9. There is a 3-letter word that has 1 syllable. This word becomes a 3-syllable word when 1 more letter is added to it. What is the 3-letter word? *Hint: it starts with an a.*

NUMBERS

1. How many bricks does it take to complete a wall that is 20 bricks long by 15 bricks tall?

2. The teacher told her students to multiply 5 numbers. After she had called out only 1 of the 5 numbers, Grace shouted the correct answer, and it was not a lucky guess. How is this possible?

3. How is 7 different from the rest of the numbers between 1 and 10?

4. How long is the answer to this question.

5. What is half of 2 + 2?

6. I have 8 marbles in a bag. I give 2 to Conor, 2 to Ezra, 2 to Eli and 2 to Anna. At the end there are still 2 marbles in the bag. How is this possible?

7. What number, when it is spelt out, has its letters in alphabetical order?

8. The candle stubs left after burning 10 candles will make 1 new candle if you melt the stubs together. If you burned 100 candles, how many new candles could you make?

DATES

1. What can you see in the middle of March and April that can't be seen at the beginning or end of either month?

2. Which month has 28 days?

3. If it takes 4 men 24 hours to build a wall, how long will it take 1 man to build the same wall?

4. Can you name (in English) 3 days that come in a row, without mentioning Tuesday, Thursday or Sunday?

5. The day before yesterday Jane was 18. Next year she will be 21. How is this possible?

6. Brian made a fake ID on his sixteenth birthday. He gave himself the birthdate of 31 September 1994, which made him 18 and the legal age to go into a pub. When he was stopped to have his ID checked, a comb and a stick of chewing gum fell out of his pocket. The doorman realised it was a fake ID. What gave Brian away?

7. Andy is 10 years old in 1850, but is only 5 years old in 1855. How is this possible?

GAMES

1. There are 5 brothers in a room. They are all occupied. Ruairí's cooking, Eugene is playing chess, Joe is reading a book and Ronan is doing the laundry. What is the fifth brother doing?

2. Ellen bought a hockey stick for her daughter. When she got home, she realised it was too tall so she had to cut it down. She cut a piece off but it was too short. She then cut off another piece to make the hockey stick just right. How is this possible?

3. Sam says he can throw a ball as hard as he can and have it stop, change direction and finally come back to him. He claims the ball will not bounce or hit off anything and he will not use string or magnets or any props. How is this possible?

4. Where can you finish a book without finishing a sentence?

5. What will not break if you throw it off the roof of the highest building in the world but will fall apart if you drop it in the ocean? (There is more than 1 answer).

6. What can you hold in your right hand but never in your left hand?

7. A man goes to a party and says that he will be home for sunrise. Before he goes he is clean-shaven, but when he returns he has a full beard. How is this possible?

8. One night, after the sun went down, Frank and Ann were in the living room reading their books. Frank said he was going to bed and he turned the only light off. Ann continued to read in the room. How is this possible if she did not have any light?

TRAVEL

1. Alice is flying to Spain and she is in first class. How is this possible if she has only enough money to fly economy and no one else paid for her?

2. Four men were on a boat trip. A storm rose and a gust of wind capsized the boat. The men were all thrown into the ocean. When they were rescued from the ocean, not a single man was wet. How is this possible?

3. A woman was sitting in her hotel room when there was a knock on the door. She opened the door to a man she had never seen before. He said, "Oh dear, I've made a mistake. I thought this was my room." He then left and took the elevator. The woman went into her room and immediately phoned security. What made the woman so suspicious?

4. Paddy was changing a flat tyre when the 4 nuts that secured the wheel fell down a drain and were lost. He had no spare nuts and was in the middle of nowhere. How did he manage to secure the wheel to his car and drive safely to a garage?

5. Detective Ted was passing a hotel room when he heard a voice say, "Don't shoot me, John!" Then there was a shot. The man ran into the room and saw a woman dead on the floor. On the opposite side of the room stood a doctor, a lawyer and an accountant. Detective Ted looked at them and immediately knew the doctor was guilty. How did he know?

6. Two salesmen, Mr Blyth and Mr Barry, were staying in the same room in the same hotel on the same night. During the night Mr Blyth slept soundly, but Mr Barry didn't. Mr Barry woke up Mr Blyth and then Mr Barry fell asleep immediately. Why did this happen?

7. What do you throw out when you want to use it but take in when you are finished using it?

8. You are the passenger on a helicopter that is 300 metres above the ground. The engine cuts out and won't start again but you do not crash. Why?

9. There are 2 planes. One is flying from New York to San Francisco at a speed of 500 m.p.h. The other is travelling from New York to San Francisco at a speed of 400 m.p.h. When the planes meet, which will be closer to San Francisco?

MISCELLANEOUS

1. What can you use to cut down a tree, dry your hair and see the stars with?

2. A prisoner is told, "If you tell a lie, we will shoot you. If you tell the truth, we will hang you." What can he say to save himself?

3. A doctor and a postman were both in love with the same woman, a girl named Laura. The postman had to go on a long trip that would last a week. Before he left, he gave Laura 7 apples. Why?

4. Emily's mother has 5 daughters. Four of them are named Eleven, Twelve, Thirteen and Fourteen. What is the name of the fifth daughter?

5. Harrison married 3 different women within a single month, without divorcing or separating from any of them and without any of them dying. How is this possible?

6. A window cleaner was cleaning a window on the twenty-eighth floor of a skyscraper. Suddenly he slipped and fell. He had no safety equipment and nothing to break his fall but he was not hurt at all. How is this possible?

7. Why are manholes round and not square?

8. Dr Green's home is decorated entirely in the colour green – the walls, the floors and the furniture are green. So why do you suppose she doesn't have green stairs?

9. What do you put in the ground when it's alive and take out when it's dead?

CHAPTER 2

TRICKS OF
THE MIND

The puzzles in this section will take more thought and time and are best worked on with a group of friends or family. The answers are rarely obvious, so give everyone time to figure them out, even though they rarely will.

PUZZLE 1
THE ROPE BRIDGE

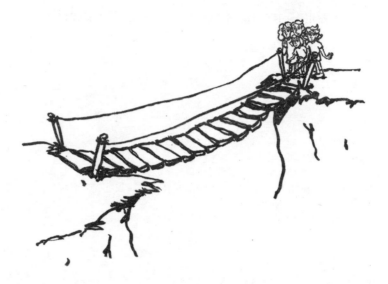

A group of 4 people must walk across a rope bridge at night. There are rabid wolves who have got their scent and will reach the group in 17 minutes, so the entire group must get across the bridge within 17 minutes. Only 2 people can cross at a time and the group only have 1 torch, which means 1 of the people must come back with the torch, as you cannot cross the bridge without light.

Each of the 4 people can cross the bridge at different speeds. One person takes 1 minute to cross, another takes 2 minutes to cross, another takes 5 minutes to cross, and the last person has been injured and takes 10 minutes to cross. When 2 people cross together, they can only go at the speed of the slower person. For example, if the 1-minute and 10-minute people cross together, it will take them 10 minutes to get to the other side. Each time 2 people cross, someone must return with the torch, until all 4 people have made it to the other side. How does everyone get across within 17 minutes, before the wolves reach them?

PUZZLE 2

CHICKEN AND FOX

You have a chicken, a fox and a bag of grain. You must cross a river with only 1 of them at a time. If you leave the fox with the chicken, it will eat the chicken, but if you leave the chicken with the grain, it will eat the grain. How is it possible to get all 3 safely across to the other side of the river?

PUZZLE 3
LIFT PROBLEM

A man lives on the nineteenth floor of an apartment building. Every day he takes the elevator down to the ground floor to go to work. When he returns, he takes the elevator to the eleventh floor and then climbs the stairs to reach his apartment. If it is raining, he does the same thing except he takes the elevator to the sixteenth floor before climbing the stairs to his apartment. He hates climbing the stairs, so why does he do it?

PUZZLE 4
FIVE QUESTIONS

Tell your friend you will ask them 5 questions and the only thing they have to do is *not* say yes or no.

Most people will think this is not very hard but you have a trick up your sleeve.

Question 1: People say you are very annoying. Do you agree with them?

They will obviously not say yes or no, but they may not like the question!

Question 2: People say that you almost never shower and prefer a natural body smell regardless of what anyone else thinks. Is this true?

Again, they will avoid saying yes or no.

Question 3: I believe you owe me money. Is that right? If you say anything but yes or no, I will take it that you do.

Again, they will think of a way to avoid using yes or no.

Now, quickly say to them: "That's 4 questions so far, isn't it?"

Most people think this is the trick, so they pause and say, "I'm not sure" or "I don't believe so."

Now you throw your hands in the air and say, "Well done! You've heard this puzzle before, haven't you?" You'll be amazed by how many people say "No!"

And that's the fifth question, so they lose. Gotcha!

PUZZLE 5
ALL THE NUMBERS

Give someone the numbers: 0, 1, 2, 3, 4, 5, 6, 7, 8, 9.

Ask them to use every digit only once to write down 2 fractions that add up to 1. So all 10 numbers must to be arranged on one side of an equal sign with another number 1 on the other side.

$$^{??}/_{??} + {}^{???}/_{???} = 1$$

HINT
It starts with $^{35}/_{70}$

PUZZLE 6
2 DOORS, 1 QUESTION

This is one of the first brain teasers I ever heard. You are faced with 2 doors. There is a guard at each door. One door is the entrance to the most wondrous place of your dreams. Behind the other door is something that will kill you. You're told that 1 guard always tells the truth and the other guard always lies. However, you don't know which guard is which. You are only allowed to ask 1 question to either of the guards and then you must walk through 1 of the 2 doors. What question should you ask to make sure you pick the right door?

PUZZLE 7
THE 5 HATS

A teacher comes into her classroom and tells her students she wants to teach them logic by setting them a challenge.

The teacher takes 5 hats out of a bag - 3 black hats and 2 white hats. She has 3 students sit in chairs lined up in a row so that the student in the back of the line can see the 2 students in front of him, the student in the middle can see the student in front of him, and the student at the front can see nothing but the classroom wall.

The teacher places a hat on the head of each student while they are blindfolded and she hides the extra 2 hats. She asks the student at the back of the line, "What colour hat do you have on?" He says he does not know. She asks the student in the middle, and he also says he doesn't know. When the teacher asks the student in the front of the line what colour hat he has, he pauses for a while and then answers correctly. What colour hat did he have on, and how did he know?

HINT

Pretend that you are the student in the back of the line. What do you see? Then pretend you are the student in the middle of the line.

PUZZLE 8
FUNNY MATHS

Split a group into 2 and write out on a piece of paper the same mathematical puzzle but show the first one to one group and the second one to the other group. Tell them they won't be able to guess the correct answer but in 5 seconds they must shout out what they think is *close* to the right answer.

Write the sum below on a piece of paper and show it to group 1.

$$1 \times 2 \times 3 \times 4 \times 5 \times 6 \times 7 \times 8$$

Write the sum below on a piece of paper and show it to group 2.

$$8 \times 7 \times 6 \times 5 \times 4 \times 3 \times 2 \times 1$$

Once they have given their guesses write down the 2 answers - now look at the answers page to reveal something interesting.

PUZZLE 9
CARD TURN

This is a famous logic test from the 1960s.

You are presented with 4 cards and you are told that all cards that have letters on one side have numbers on the other.

You are now presented with a statement: If a card has a vowel on one side, it must have an even number on the other side.

Then ask your friend this question:

What is the fewest number of cards that you need to turn over to find out whether the statement above is true and which card (or cards) are they?

PUZZLE 10
CARD DISTRACTION

You are in a game of cards with 3 other people and you are dealing a regular set of 52 cards. The cards are dealt clockwise one at a time to each player until everyone has 13 cards each and all the cards are dealt. However, in the middle of your deal you are distracted and you forget where you have got to in dealing the cards. None of the other players can remember either. How can you immediately resume the deal without counting how many cards each player has?

PUZZLE 11
A FUNNY EQUATION

How do you make the following equation correct without writing anything else on the page?

$$8 + 8 = 91$$

PUZZLE 12
COINS ON A TABLE

A 10-cent piece sits on the kitchen table. Harry tells his sister that he can put a 5-cent piece under the 10-cent piece without lifting it or touching it in any way. How can he do this?

PUZZLE 13
TWO BIBLES

A man took an antique King James Bible to get it valued. He needed a lot of money very quickly so he wanted to sell it. The antique dealer told him it was worth €1 million but that if it were the only remaining copy, it would be worth 10 times that amount. Sadly the dealer knew there was 1 more copy in the world. The owner of the Bible took his treasured possession home and burnt it in the fire. Why?

PUZZLE 14
BRAIN MELT

If you have a group of people in the room, ask them to pair off and face each other. Tell them that the goal is to answer the 2 questions quicker than the person they are sitting opposite, so it is a test of quick thinking.

When they are ready, tell them you will ask the 2 questions very quickly one after the other.

Question 1: What colour is your fridge? (Ask Question 2 without pausing)

Question 2: What do cows drink?

You will find that nearly everyone shouts out "milk" to Question 2. The correct answer is water!

You can also do the same trick on 1 person by asking them to say the word "silk" 10 times quickly and then asking them: What does a cow drink?

PUZZLE 15
EYES OPEN

Show the puzzle below to your friend and ask them how good their brain power and eyesight are.

Can you find the the mistake? You only have 30 seconds.

1, 2, 3, 4, 5, 6, 7, 8, 9, 10, 11, 12, 13, 14, 15, 16

PUZZLE 16
GHOST WORD

Show the word below to your friends and tell them you will give them 3 chances to pronounce it correctly and see how they do.

GHOTI

PUZZLE 17
12 ORANGES

How do you divide 12 oranges equally between 13 children? Each child should get the exact same amount.

PUZZLE 18
WORD SHRINK

"Startling" is a 9-letter word and it becomes a different word every time you remove 1 letter from it, right up to when there is a single letter remaining. See if you can work out what the words are from 8 letters to just 1 letter.

STARTLING

PUZZLE 19
A THOUSAND EIGHTS

I am giving you 8 number 8's and you can use any equation you want to make them into a sum that equals exactly 1,000. You must use all the 8's and you can add, subtract, multiply or divide.

8, 8, 8, 8, 8, 8, 8, 8

PUZZLE 20
THE MISSING LETTER

Show someone this 4-letter word with 1 letter missing and ask them to guess what the missing letter is and what word it would make.

_ANY

This will seem very easy to them and they will say "Many" straight away.

Now it is up to you to say the word "many" a few times out loud and then show them the second 4-letter word with 1 letter missing:

_ENY

Ask them if they can name the missing letter in 10 seconds. Tell them many people can't get this one. *Many* people!

PUZZLE 21
FIND THE ERRORS

Ask someone if they are any good at basic spelling and grammar. Most people will say yes. Show the text below to them and get them to point out the 5 errors.

There are are five things wrong
with this sentence; only really
smart people will be able to
to figure out the misteaks

PUZZLE 22
15 MINUTES

You have an 11-minute hourglass and a 7-minute hourglass. You need to measure exactly 15 minutes. How do you do it?

PUZZLE 23
OPTIMIST OR PESSIMIST?

Show the word below to a friend and ask them how they would pronounce it.

OPPORTUNITYISNOWHERE

PUZZLE 24
TWO HORSES

A very odd but rich man had 2 sons. He always felt they should prove themselves to him, so on his deathbed he set them a challenge, and the winner would inherit his entire fortune.

He bought 2 horses, one for each son, and put them in a stable 50 miles from the family's mansion. He told his 2 sons that they must race the horses back to the mansion, but the challenge was that the winner was the person whose horse finished second. He also told them the winner could not share the fortune with his brother.

The 2 sons set out, each determined to win the inheritance. They kept trying to get the other to start riding his horse. Finally they came across a wise woman and they asked her for advice. After the woman spoke to them, they immediately raced the horses back to the mansion as fast as they could.

What did the wise woman say?

PUZZLE 25
RACE CAR TIME

There is a famous car race in which a team of 2 drivers must drive the course one after the other in the same car. The course is very tricky, with lots of hills, forests, streams and bridges. It finishes in the same place as it starts. The first person tackles the course, and when they get to the finish line they get out of the car and the second racer gets in. The second racer's goal is to finish as close as possible to the time of their teammate. No clocks, watches or other timepieces are allowed. Drivers are not permitted to speak with anyone as they drive. A team figured out a way to ensure they won by finishing in almost exactly the same time over a 4-minute race. How did they do it?

PUZZLE 26
MYSTERY HOUR

There is 1 hour of the year when there has never been a road traffic accident in Ireland or in the UK. In fact almost nothing has ever happened during this hour. Can you work out when it is?

PUZZLE 27
UNIQUE WORDS

Show a friend these 8 words and tell them the words all have something very obvious in common. But what is it?

Assess

Banana

Dresser

Grammar

Potato

Revive

Uneven

Voodoo

PUZZLE 28
STRANGER DANGER

Grace and Lucy's car broke down and they knocked on a stranger's door for help. Little did they know the person in the house was a madman who wanted to poison both of them. He gave both Lucy and Grace a cold drink of lemonade with ice. Lucy was thirsty and drank 2 glasses very quickly, while Grace drank hers slowly. Grace died but Lucy did not. Why?

CHAPTER 3
OUTSMART
OTHERS

Here are tricks, challenges and impossible questions
that will confound even the cleverest of your friends
and family. It might even help you win the odd bet or
two.

UNLOCK YOUR ARMS

THE CHALLENGE

This is a great trick to use on a crowd of people; the more the better.

Ask everyone to face you and follow your lead as you have a task that will show if they are creative or not.

Tell them to hold their arms out straight in front of them with the back of their hands facing each other and their palms facing outwards, as in the diagram below.

Now ask them to cross their arms so they interlock their fingers and keep their arms straight.

Ask everyone to look down to see if their left finger or their right finger is on top of their hands.

Now tell everyone that the question of which finger is on top is not the real challenge. The challenge is to uncross their arms without taking their hands apart.

You will be able to do it but they will not!

THE TRICK

When you ask people to look down at their hands to see which finger is on top, you take your hands apart and interlock them in the normal way. Do this quickly so no one sees you and then just twist your wrists so it looks like you are back in the same position as everyone else (even though you are not). It is now easy for you to just turn your arms back. But for anyone else it's impossible.

MAGIC LIPSTICK

THE CHALLENGE

Ask to borrow some lipstick from someone. Then ask your friend to hold out their hands palms down, take their hands and separate them a bit and then ask them to hold one of their hands in a tight fist. Dot a smudge of lipstick onto the palm of your hand. Then rub the lipstick away with your finger until it has vanished. Then ask your friend to open their hand palm upwards. To their shock, they will see a smudge of lipstick on the palm of their hand!

THE TRICK

When you have the lipstick, take off the lid while casually talking to your friend (tell them they're about to see something amazing, etc). While you are talking, without them seeing, rub the tip of your index finger on the top of the lipstick, so there is a coating of lipstick on your fingertip.

Ask your friend to hold out both of their hands with

their palms facing down. Still talking, casually separate their hands with yours and say, "Just keep your hands a bit apart so that this will work." While you are separating their hands, touch your finger against their left palm to transfer the lipstick onto their hand. Then you simply say, "Close your left hand into a fist and put your other hand down." Then simply dot your hand with lipstick, rub it away and magically transfer it to their hand!

CARD CUT

THE CHALLENGE

Tell a friend you will be able to find a card they choose at random and that they will not know how you did it. Shuffle the pack of cards until your friend is happy they are well shuffled. Now ask them to cut the deck, mark the spot they cut to and have them look at that card without you seeing it. You then proceed to find it or reveal it through mindreading.

THE TRICK

This is a simple yet clever card trick. After shuffling the cards, casually glance at the bottom card. Remember it and place the deck face down on the table. Ask your friend to cut the deck in half and place the 2 halves side by side on the table. Now take the other half of the deck (the half your friend hasn't touched) and place it on top of the pile they did touch, but in a criss-cross fashion as in the diagram below.

Cut the cards   Put beside each other   Put lower half in a
                                                 criss-cross on top

Now ask your friend to look at the card they cut to. He/she will think that this is the card they picked but they are actually looking at the card that was on the bottom of the deck of cards (which is the card you have already glanced at). You now know their card, so shuffle the cards or have them shuffle them. You can then run though the deck of cards and find their card magically! Your friend won't notice how you set this up.

COIN MOVE

THE CHALLENGE

Lay out 6 coins as in the image below and tell your friend they must move only 1 coin so that there will be 4 coins in each row.

THE TRICK

The secret is to pick up the coin at the top and place it on top of the coin in the corner which is part of both rows. No one said the coins couldn't be stacked on top of each other!

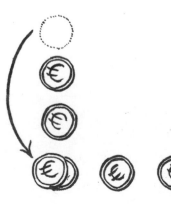

64

COIN CHALLENGE

THE CHALLENGE

Take out a 5-cent coin and ask your friend to put the coin on its side. Ask them how many coins they think they need to stack face up so that the stack is the same height as the coin on its side. Tell them if they bet €1 you'll give them €5 if they get it right, but you only get their €1 if they get it wrong. This will be very tempting!

THE TRICK

There is no trick here, really – it's more of an optical illusion. Most people say 8 to 10 coins, but in fact you need to stack between 12 and 13 5-cent coins to reach the same height as 1 coin on its side. You can actually win every time, as if they say 12, you say it's closer to 13, and if they say 13 you say it's closer to 12!

STICK PUZZLE 1

THE CHALLENGE

Set up the matchsticks as in the image below and ask your friend to move only 2 matchsticks to create 4 boxes instead of 5. There can be no loose matchsticks.

Set-up:

THE TRICK

Step 1:

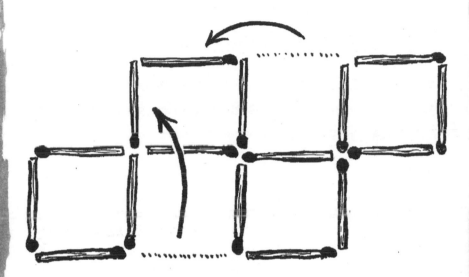

Step 2:

STICK PUZZLE 2

THE CHALLENGE

Ask your friend to take away 9 sticks to leave only 4 squares, making sure that every remaining stick forms part of a square. All squares, whether large or small, count.

Set-up:

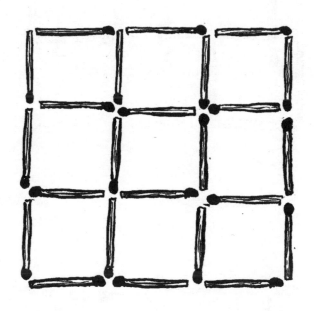

THE TRICK

It's harder than it looks!

This is what you should end up with.

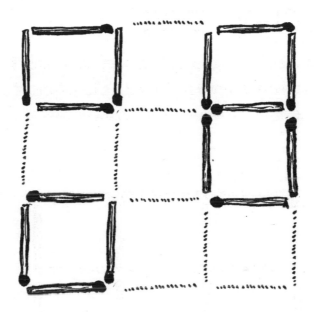

STICK PUZZLE 3

THE CHALLENGE

Give your friend 3 matchsticks. Tell them they need to make 4 out of them without breaking any.

THE TRICK

Make the sticks into the number 4.

MISSING PENCIL

THE CHALLENGE

Tell your friends you can push a pencil right through your hand. Hold out your palm, take a pencil and have 2 practice thrusts into your palm, stopping at the palm each time. Then the third time, as you shout out "Arrrghhh!" slam your hand down, and the pencil will have completely disappeared.

THE TRICK

This trick relies on your skills of distraction. First, make sure your friend is staring at your hand. Then, each time you thrust the pencil down to your palm, start the thrust from your ear. The trick is that the third time you thrust your hand down you instead put the pencil behind your ear. Make sure you are standing in a position where the pencil behind your ear is hidden from your friend. They will be looking at your hands wondering where the pencil is!

CALCULATOR TRICK

THE CHALLENGE

Look for a friend who is always on their iPhone. Tell them you will show them something amazing on their phone if they promise to put their phone away afterwards. Ask them to open their calculator app and clear all previous sums. Then ask them to type in any random 4-digit number and add it to their 4-digit PIN (or another 4-digit number they know well). Then tell them to press Equals (=). Tell them that even though they have added a random 4-digit number to their PIN, you will still be able to work out what their PIN is.

THE TRICK

This is a superb trick and is easy to do. Ask your friend to type in a random 4-digit number. Then ask them to add their 4-digit

PIN and press Equals (=). You can now ask to see the number on screen as you would have to be a mathematical genius to figure out their PIN code from that. Take your friend's phone and secretly press Clear (C) and then press Equals (=). For some reason, their 4-digit PIN will come up on screen. Memorize it and then press Clear (C) again so that the screen shows zero. Then "read their mind" and tell them their PIN.

SNAP

THE CHALLENGE

Ask a friend to think of a famous person, and with a few clicks of your fingers, another person will magically be able to guess who it is.

THE TRICK

This is a great trick for 2 people to play on a third person. It just takes a little practice. It looks like you are sending thoughts to the other person's brain, when in reality you use clues to help them guess.

You basically want to spell out the famous person's name.

To indicate a consonant, start the sentence you speak to your partner with that letter. For example, if you say "Let's go!" the other person will know the first letter is "*l*".

To indicate vowels, you snap your fingers. For "*a*" snap once. For "*e*" snap twice. Similarly, 3 times for "*i*", 4 times for "*o*", and for "*u*" snap 5 times. Make sure you can snap your fingers!

Always start by saying, "Snap *is* the name of the game" if the person is alive, and "Snap *was* the name of the game" if the person is dead. Go on speaking sentences for consonants and snapping for the vowels until your partner guesses correctly.

You can also use other tricks to help your partner guess. For example, when you put your hands on your face (as if you are thinking) it can indicate that you have finished the first name and are moving on to the surname.

Example: Kylie Jenner

Start by looking at your partner and saying, "Snap is the name of the game" (as she is alive).

Say "Kneel down."

Say "You will benefit doing this."

Say "Listen carefully."

Snap 3 times (for "i").

Put your hands on your face. At this stage they will probably know it's Kylie so you can move on to the surname without snapping for the "e".

Say "Jeepers, this is taking longer than I expected."

There is really only one famous Kylie J alive, so they will likely get it at this stage. Simple! Practise lots.

NINE-CARD TRICK

THE CHALLENGE

Amaze your friends and family with your ability to predict their chosen card every time. Lay out 9 playing cards in 3 rows of 3, face down on a table. While you have your back turned, ask a friend to choose a card, look at it and then place it face down on the table again. When you turn around you will be able to reveal which card they chose.

THE TRICK

To do this trick you need a partner. The cards are laid out on the table 3 across and 3 down. While you have your back turned, your friend simply chooses 1 card. When they do this, your partner can see which card they have chosen.

When you turn around, you look at your partner's hand. They are holding the box of cards and their thumb points to the position of the card your friend chose. The box is the same shape as the 9 cards laid out on the table. If your partner points to the middle of the box with their thumb, they are indicating that your friend chose the middle card. If they point their thumb to the top middle of the box, they are indicating the top middle card and so on.

TOOTHPICK DISAPPEARANCE

THE CHALLENGE

Show your friends how you can make a toothpick disappear and see if they can work out how you did it.

THE TRICK

This takes a little bit of work beforehand but it's a remarkably fun trick and very easy to do, with just a little practice. Stick a toothpick to the outside of your thumb with some sticky tape. The toothpick should be parallel with your thumb (like in the image) and hidden when you give someone the thumbs up.

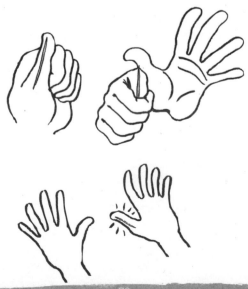

Ensure everyone is sitting or standing directly in front of you. Hold up the toothpick with your thumb bent and your fingers wrapped around it. It will just look like you are holding a toothpick in your hand.

Now with your other hand go to grab the toothpick. While it is hidden from view open your hand so your palm is facing your audience. They will see you no longer have the toothpick and will presume it is in your other hand. Then open your other hand and reveal that the toothpick has disappeared! You can also reverse the trick to make the toothpick reappear.

PREDICT THE NUMBER

THE CHALLENGE

Tell your friend that you will show them a mind-boggling trick on an iPhone if they promise to put their device away afterwards. Ask your friend for a 2-digit number and type it into your iPhone using the calculator app. Then give your friend your phone. Ask them to multiply this number by any 3-digit number and then multiply their answer by a 4-digit number. Tell them to press equals. Ask them if they think there is any way you could know the number on the screen. They will believe this is impossible as they have freely picked the numbers. Amaze them by taking out of your pocket a piece of paper with the correct number written on it!

THE TRICK

Write down any 9-digit number in the phone and also on a piece of paper in advance.

Put the piece of paper in your pocket.

Now tap the Plus key (+).

Tap Zero (0).

Tap Multiply (×).

Tap Open Bracket (which you can only tap if you have the phone turned sideways.

Tap Clear (C).

The phone should read zero but you will notice the multiplication sign (×) is highlighted.

So when you ask your friend for a 2-digit number and type it in, everything looks normal. Then hand them the phone so they can multiply it by a 3-digit number of their choosing and then multiply the answer by a 4-digit number. Because of how you set up the phone at the beginning, once your friend presses Equals (=) it will give the number you had put in at the start! To your friend's amazement, you will have that number written down!

SHOW OF STRENGTH

THE CHALLENGE

Look your friend in the eyes and tell them you will be able to lift them in the air using just your arms but they won't be able to do the same to you. You need to pick someone bigger than you so they will think that if you can do it they will definitely be able to do it.

THE TRICK

Facing your friend, straighten your arms and put them underneath their armpits. Instruct them to keep their arms straight and by their side. Now get another friend to kneel down behind your first friend and have them push up your arms and wrists to lift your first friend off the ground.

Once they return to the ground have your friend silently walk away. Your friend will not be able to lift you when they try. You will need to be sure your second friend is very quiet, or you may need to talk loudly or grunt with effort to ensure your friend cannot hear the person behind them.

-

RED SIX AND NINE

THE CHALLENGE

Open a pack of cards and take out the 6 of diamonds and the 9 of hearts. Hand the cards to a friend and ask them to put the cards into the middle of the pack. They can put the 2 cards in different places if they like. Tap on the top of the deck and move your hand around the deck of cards. Then throw the deck of cards on the table, shouting your favourite magic word, and the 6 of diamonds and 9 of hearts will be left in your hand, much to the shock of your friend.

THE TRICK

The trick is that the 2 cards left in your hand are actually the 6 *of hearts* and the *9 of diamonds* (not the 6 of diamonds and the 9 of hearts, but most people don't notice this). You place the 6 of hearts and 9 of diamonds at the top and the bottom of the pack in advance. After your friend has put their 2 cards back in the pack, squeeze the top and bottom cards so that the rest of the cards fall onto the table but these 2 remain in your hand.

If you find this too difficult, just put the 2 cards at the top of the deck. Tap the pack and lift these 2 cards off and reveal them to your astonished friend.

NOTE

This is a trick you can really do only once before your friend notices what's going on.

RUBBER BAND JUMP

THE CHALLENGE

Show your friends how you can make a rubber band jump from 2 fingers to the next 2 fingers. Place the rubber band on 2 fingers and show everyone. Open your hand and then the rubber band will have magically transferred to your other 2 fingers!

THE TRICK

This trick is all about the set-up. Put the rubber band on your fingers as shown below, with the other side of the band against all 4 of the tips of your fingers. When you flick the tips of your fingers the rubber band pops over to the other 2 fingers. It's that simple!

NAPKIN TOSS

THE CHALLENGE

When you are at dinner, tell the person beside you that you can make a napkin disappear. Take your napkin, scrunch it up and stand up beside the person, while they remain sitting down. Ask them to put out their hand and smash the napkin down on their hand once, then twice, and then on the third time as you smash your hand down, the napkin has disappeared.

THE TRICK

When you stand up, make sure you stand beside the person and not in front of them. Tell them to focus on their hand so that they are looking down or straight ahead. They won't be looking up, which is what's important.

The third time your hand goes in the air, you just throw the napkin behind the chair. It is such a simple trick, but the person in the chair is always astonished.

This is a trick that only works on 1 person - everyone else at the table will know what has happened. This is always funny for the group as they are in on the trick.

HELLO MR PERFECT

THE CHALLENGE

Take out a pack of cards and tell your friend that they are free to pick any card. Then phone a friend called Mr Perfect, a magician you know, who will be able to read your mind through the phone. Obviously, this sounds impossible. After your friend picks a card, ring Mr Perfect and after a few words with him, pass the phone to the person who picked the card and Mr Perfect will say their card to them.

THE TRICK

To set up this trick with your friend, change their name in your phone to Mr Perfect.

Let's say the person you are tricking is called John and he chose the 9 of hearts.

Then you phone your partner and say, "Hello, Mr Perfect."

Once your partner hears this, they start speaking into the phone: "2, 3, 4, 5, 6, 7, 8, 9, 10, Jack, Queen, King, Ace." The moment they reach the number 9 (as that's the number of the card John chose), you say, "I am going to hand the phone over to John now."

When Mr Perfect hears you speak, he now knows it is the number 9, so he then says, "Spades, clubs, hearts, diamonds."

As soon he says "Hearts", you say "OK" and hand over the phone to John.

Mr Perfect now knows the card is the 9 of hearts!

John will be completely spooked!

Practise this one with your friend a few times first and have Mr Perfect speak slowly and quietly into the phone.

KNOT TIE

THE CHALLENGE

Ask your friend if they can tie a knot in a piece of string without ever letting go of either end of the string. This will seem impossible ... until you do it!

THE TRICK

Lay out the string on the table. Fold your arms so that one of your hands rests on top of your arm and the other hand sits under the armpit. It does not matter which hand does which.

While in this position, lean forward and pick up the string with your hands in this position. Using the hand under your armpit, you will easily be able to pick up one end of the string, while you will have to stretch the hand resting on your arm a little to grab the other end.

Once you have an end of the string in each hand, uncross your arms and there will be a knot in the string. Easy!

NAPKIN TEAR

THE CHALLENGE

This is another good napkin trick. Take a paper napkin and twist it so it is rolled up completely. Then ask your friend if they can rip the napkin in half. Challenge them by saying that you can do it, so they should be able to!

THE TRICK

While your friend is trying to tear their napkin, secretly put your thumbs in water. Ask them to give you their napkin and put your thumbs in the centre of the napkin to wet it (without them seeing). This will make it much easier to tear. While you are tearing, you may need to twist the napkin a little too.

CARD ILLUSION

THE CHALLENGE

This is a great optical illusion. All you need is a pack of cards and a paper clip. Hold up 5 cards to your friend so that they can see which card each one is, like in the diagram below. Then turn the cards around so that they are facing you, and place a paperclip on the middle card. Ask your friend to tell you which card the paper clip is on. They will rarely get it right.

THE TRICK

Try this yourself. You think it's on the middle card but in fact when you turn the cards around, the paperclip is on the first card.

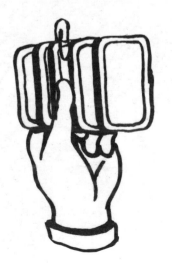 

LEG SWING

THE CHALLENGE

Tell a friend that you don't think they are able to control their legs. They will obviously disagree. Put them in a sitting position and tell them all they have to do is raise their right leg and turn it in a clockwise direction. They will be able to do this. Now ask them to continue doing this and with their right hand draw the number 6 in the air with their finger. Suddenly their leg will be going in the opposite direction!

THE TRICK

There is no trick here - it is just very hard to control your leg when you're making a figure of 6 with your finger. Some would say it's impossible but in fact I did see someone do it once! Her name was Isobel.

HYPNOTISE HANDS

THE CHALLENGE

Hypnotise a person so that they cannot move their fingers however hard they try. Put their elbows on the table and ask them to place their hands together, as if in prayer. Tell them to spread out their fingers. Next ask them to bend their middle fingers inwards so they cross (see diagram below). Pick up a piece of paper, fold it, and slide it between your friend's fourth fingers. Now do some chanting, sing a song or make some loud noises - whatever you like. Finish by counting back from 5 to 0 and then say, "Please release your fingers so the piece of paper falls to the floor. Before they try to obey your instruction, demonstrate what you mean - make sure your fingers are in the prayer position but without your middle fingers bent. They won't be able to do it.

THE TRICK

There is no real trick! When your fingers are in this position, it is impossible to separate your ring fingers. Just make sure your friend doesn't cheat by sliding their fingers sideways so that the paper falls.

TRIANGLE PROBLEM

THE CHALLENGE

Ask your friend how many triangles they can make out of 6 matches. Give them 3 minutes to do the task and tell them you will definitely make more triangles then they can. The rules are that you cannot add any more matches (or anything else), you cannot break any matches and all the triangles must be the same size. Your friend will likely be able to make only 2 triangles.

THE TRICK

This trick is easiest if you do it on a table with a tablecloth on it. Lay out the first triangle and then create a pyramid. You will have created 4 triangles.

RIP AN APPLE

THE CHALLENGE

Tell your friend that you can rip an apple in two with your bare hands. They definitely won't believe you. Ask them to try first.

THE TRICK

You do need to practice this one and also have a little bit of strength, so it's not for the youngest tricksters.

First, secretly use your nail to break the skin of the apple in a straight line around the entire apple. When you have an audience, hide the rip in the skin with your fingers and then hold the apple on each side. Pull very hard while twisting one half clockwise and the other half anticlockwise and the apple will rip neatly in half. This can be tricky but it's worth it!

CORK IN A GLASS

THE CHALLENGE

Fill a glass with water and ask a friend if they can get a cork to stay in the middle of the glass and not move to the edge. Of course they won't be able to do it.

THE TRICK

The trick is to fill the glass to the brim until it is almost spilling over the top. When the water is just above the rim of the glass, the cork will move to the centre and stay there. Hey presto!

STICKY DICE

THE CHALLENGE

Take 3 dice and ask your friend if they think it's possible to balance 2 of them on top of the other die. Let them have a go and then show them that you can do it. Don't tell them how, though!

THE TRICK

Without your friend seeing, wet your fingertips with water or your tongue and then stick 2 of the dice together. It's best to stick together the numbers 2, 4 or 6 because these faces have no middle spot and that makes it easier. Once you have done this the dice will stick for a little while. Now it's just a matter of balancing them on top of the single die. What is also good is that when the dice fall apart it's not easy to see any moisture on them.

COIN PASS

THE CHALLENGE

Challenge a friend to pass a 20-cent coin through a piece of paper with a hole the size of a 5-cent coin in it. They are not allowed to tear the paper. When they get frustrated show them how it is done.

THE TRICK

Take a piece of paper and place a 5-cent coin on it. Draw around the 5-cent coin and carefully cut out a circle. Fold the paper in half and drop the 20-cent coin into the hole. It won't go though. Now, bend the top corners of the piece of paper inwards and the 20-cent coin will pass through the hole!

CHAPTER 4
HILARIOUS JOKES

No book that challenges the mind should ignore the funny bone. This chapter contains some of the best and the corniest jokes that will have people laughing and groaning in equal measure.

What's green and not very heavy?

Light green.

I got into a fight with 1, 3, 5, 7 and 9.

The odds were against me.

My dad wants me to get a donor card.

He's a man after my own heart.

A book just fell on my head.

I've only got my shelf to blame.

I bought a can of fly spray from the supermarket today.

I sprayed it all over myself and I still can't fly.

What's a foot long, made of leather and sounds like a sneeze?

A shoe.

What did the drummer name his daughters?

Anna 1, Anna 2!

What is a clock's favourite time of day?

6.30. Hands down.

How does the moon cut the sun's hair?

Eclipse it.

Some guy stopped me in the street and asked, "Why are you carrying a 9-foot book?"

I replied, "It's a long story."

What do you call a Frenchman with sandals?

Phillipe Flop.

A Roman walks into a bar, holds up 2 fingers, and says, "Five beers, please."

Why do scuba divers always fall backwards out of the boat?

Because if they fell forwards, they'd still be in the boat.

There is a saying: whatever you do in life, always give 100%.

I think they might want to reconsider that if they are donating blood.

Some guy just assaulted me with milk, cream and butter.

How dairy!

I asked my friend about a puppet-making factory.

He said he could pull a few strings.

The inventor of the lozenge died.

There will be no coughin' at the funeral.

Why can't you hear a pterodactyl going to the bathroom?

Because the P is silent.

What is big, grey and unimportant?

An irrelephant.

I put up a high-voltage fence around my property.

My neighbour is dead against it.

*I always felt my twin brother was my parents' favourite. I think
I realised it when they asked me to blow up all the balloons for
his surprise party!*

How many Irish mothers does it take to change a light bulb?

None. They're happy to sit in the dark.

What do you call a priest on a motorbike?

Rev.

What do you call a guy who has been slow-cooked for a long time?

Stu.

My son is worried about being bullied in school because of his name. I said, "Don't be silly, Someoneyourownsize, you'll be fine!"

I broke up with my last boyfriend because he wouldn't stop counting.

I wonder what he's up to now.

My daughter asked me to make a ballerina costume.

I didn't know where to start but then I put two and two together.

Interviewer: "Are you a good waiter?"

Waiter: "Well, I do bring a lot to the table."

My dad always said the sky is the limit.

That's why he got fired from NASA.

Why don't ants get sick?

Because they have small anty bodies.

Why did the lifeguard not save the hippy?

Because he was too far out, man.

What do you call a fat psychic?

A 4-chin teller

Did you hear what happened to the inventor of the knock-knock joke?

He won the no bell prize!

I ate 3 bowls of alphabet soup last night.

This morning I had a huge vowel movement.

Patient: "Doctor, I have a poo every morning at 8 a.m."

Doctor: "What is wrong with that?"

Patient: "I wake up at 9."

What's worse than finding a worm in your apple?

Finding half a worm.

I just started my own cloning business.

I love being my own boss.

I once dated a girl who was a twin and people used to ask me how I told them apart.

I told them that Mia always wore green nail varnish and Cillian was a man.

Did you hear about the 2 guys who stole a calendar?

They each got 6 months.

Where do pirates shop?

SPARRRRR!

How do you make Lady Gaga mad?

Poke her face.

I tried to teach my dog to dance.

But it didn't work out. He has 2 left feet.

A sandwich walks into a bar.

The barman says, "I'm sorry but we don't serve sandwiches."

What do you call a boomerang that won't come back?

A stick.

What's the difference between broccoli and bogies?

Kids will eat bogies.

My boss told me to have a great day.

So I left and went home!

What did the buffalo say when his son left for school?

"Bison."

What do English teachers say to each other at conferences?

"Haven't we metaphor?"

Why do nurses carry a red pen?

In case they need to draw blood.

I just left my job as I couldn't work for my boss after what he said to me.

What did he say to you?

"You're fired!"

What did the green grape say to the purple grape?

"Breathe."

Knock, knock.

Who's there?

Smell Mop.

Smell Mop who?

(Think about it. Yuk!)

Man: "It's a fancy dress party. I'm dressed as a harp."

Wife: "You're too small to be a harp."

Man: "Are you calling me a lyre?"

A man looks in mirror and says, "Oh my goodness, I've put on a lot of weight and I am losing my hair. That's not good."

Mum whispers to her daughter, "Go on, pay your dad a compliment."

The daughter says, "Well, Dad, your eyesight is still very good."

A wife sends a text to her husband: "Windows frozen!"

Her husband replies: "Just pour some warm water over it."

Then the wife sends back: "The computer's totally broken now!"

What is a fear of giants called?

Fee-Fi-Phobia.

Why was the sand wet?

Because the sea-weed.

ONE MEN MAY LIKE MORE:

A man walks into a doctor's office and says, "Doc, my brother's crazy! He thinks he's a chicken."

The doctor says, "Why don't you bring him in?"

The man says, "I would, but I need the eggs."

ONE WOMEN MAY LIKE MORE:

Two women are speaking to each other. The first says, "My husband is an angel."

The other responds: "You're lucky. My husband is still alive."

ONE KIDS MAY LIKE MORE:

A boy was spending too much time on his Xbox.

His dad said, "Son, when Abe Lincoln was your age, he was studying books by the light of the fireplace."

The son thought about this for a moment and replied, "Dad, when Abe Lincoln was your age, he was the President of the United States!"

CHAPTER 5

WAYS TO BE THE CENTRE OF ATTENTION

The following chapter will have everyone huddled around with challenging questions that provide amusement, hilarity and lots of amazement.

Questions to Divide the Room

Have you ever felt certain about the answer to a question and then suddenly found that not everyone agrees? Ask a group these questions one by one but make everyone write down their answers before revealing them. You'll be surprised by the results.

» Are tennis balls green or yellow?

» Do you eat breakfast then brush your teeth or brush your teeth then eat breakfast?

» Do you cut toast into triangles or rectangles?

» Do you fold or scrunch the toilet paper?

» Which way should toilet paper sit on the holder, over or under?

» In the word SCENT (spell it out), would you say the S or the C is the silent letter?

» Is it OK to put milk into tea while the teabag is still in the cup?

» Do you button a shirt bottom to top or top to bottom?

» Is it wrong to pee in the shower?

» Which do you prefer, chocolate or vanilla ice cream?

» Do you shower mainly facing the shower head or facing away from it? (Most people turn around but you have to choose which side you spend more time on.)

» Which character in *Friends* would you get rid of, Ross or Phoebe?

» Should pineapple be a pizza topping?

» Marzipan - yum or yuk?

» Crocs - great invention or not in a million years?

This exercise highlights that everyone has a different perspective. There is always a person in the group who challenges each answer and tries to come up with a third one. Who is that in your family?

Would You Rather?

Not everyone has the same views on jobs, superpowers or even how much risk they are comfortable with. Ask a group the questions below to see if you can work out more about your family and friends.

Would you rather:

» Be immortal or be guaranteed to die at 69? (Think about it!)

» Be crisp-free or chocolate-free for the rest of your life?

» Be poor and work at a job you love or be rich and work at a job you hate?

» Have no taste buds or be colour blind?

» From the age of 21, be blind or be deaf?

» Be 10 minutes late or 10 minutes early for everything?

» Have the superpower of invisibility or be able to fly?

» Have 3 arms or 3 legs?

» Have a stomach ache or have a headache?

» Go forward or back in time?

» Be 4 ft 7" in height or 7 ft 4" in height?

» Have a guaranteed €100,000 or a 50/50 chance at winning €750,000?

» Have unlimited international first-class travel on any airline or never have to pay for meals at restaurants?

» Never lose your phone again or never lose your keys again?

» Lose your left hand or your right foot?

» Look 10 years older from the neck up or the neck down?

» Be the funniest person in the room or the most intelligent?

» Have €5,000 every month for the rest of your life or €1 million today?

» Never eat meat again or have to work in a slaughterhouse for 3 months?

» Be locked for a week in a room that is always dark or always bright?

» Wake up in the middle of a desert or wake up in a rowboat in the middle of the ocean?

The Ultimatum Game

If you are worried about robots taking over the world, this game might give you some hope. It proves that we humans are not very rational and that it will take robots a long time to figure out what makes us tick! You need 2 people to play the game, as well as yourself as the banker. You tell the first person you are going to ask them a question and you must accept their first response. The second person can only respond yes or no to what they are offered.

The offer

I will give you €20 on 1 condition: you must give some of the money to the other person. It is up to you how much you keep and how much you give away. You cannot talk to each other about your decision. You can split the money any way you like (e.g. €10/€10; €15/€5; €19/€1) and the other person can either accept or reject the deal. If they accept the deal, you both get the money. But if they reject the deal, neither of you get any money.

Let them know there are no second chances and that there can be no bargaining after the deal has been accepted or rejected. Their first decision is final.

Before you read on, ask yourself how much you would offer the other person.

THE INTERESTING PART

Often people say they will offer the other person €10, and the other person almost always accepts. Why would they not?

If this happens, you step in and play the game. Say you will offer them €1 and you will keep €19. Almost always, they reject the offer. If they think about it they have just lost €1, as the only options were to accept that amount or receive nothing at all.

The reason it is usually rejected is that we don't think it's a fair deal. A robot would accept 1 cent, even if the other person kept €19.99, as it is rational to accept something over nothing!

Try this game on different groups and see what results you get.

SHARE THE WEALTH

This is a fun experimental game you can play with any number of players sitting around a table. Give everyone 10 identical coins (or poker chips that represent money) and say you are going to play a game. Everyone is to put a number of their coins into a hat in the middle of the table. The amount each person will put in is a secret only known to them. They can contribute anything from zero to 10 coins.

Once everyone has done this, 1 person will count all the coins in the hat and whatever the total is, they will double the amount and share the coins out equally between everyone. So, for example, if you had 5 players and they all put in all their coins, then 50 coins would be in the hat and you would double this to 100. Then everyone would get an equal amount back, which would be 20 coins. This is a happy outcome for everyone.

However, if 4 people put in 10 coins each and 1 person put in none, you would have 40 coins in the hat. You double this to 80, which is equally shared between the 5 people. Everyone gets 16 coins back. This means 4 players get 16 coins but the player who put nothing in has 16 coins plus his original 10 - 26 coins in total.

Knowing what you know now - and wanting both yourself and everyone else to do well in the game - how many coins would you put in? Play the game at least twice to see what choices people make.

How Much Do We Know?

There are lots of things out there that we hear and pass every day but do we actually know what they are? Test a group of family and friends with these.

- » What exactly is a macchiato?

- » The letter a: why do we write it like this: a and type it like this: a?

- » Who becomes President in the USA if the President and Vice President are killed?

- » Why did Pluto get its planet status revoked?

- » Are humans the only animals that cry?

- » How does Wi-Fi work?

- » Were humans always awkward? Do you think cavemen were and if not when did we become awkward?

- » How would you describe a colour without pointing to it or using its name?

- » Can you explain the difference between left and right to someone from a different planet?

There are no answers to these at the back of the book. It's up to you to work it out or see how much the group actually knows.

FAMOUS INTERVIEW QUESTION

This is a famous job interview question. You are driving in a 2-seater car on a cold evening. You come upon a bus stop where you see 3 people waiting for the bus. The first is your best friend from school, who you have not seen for 15 years. The second is the partner of your dreams, the person you always wanted to meet. The third is a sick old lady who needs to get to the hospital. Knowing there is room for only 1 passenger in your car, what do you do?

Ask everyone around the table and see who comes up with the best answer. There is a very good answer in the answers section but don't peek until everyone has given their answer!

THE PARENTING DILEMMA

You are a parent with 3 children. One day there is a knock at the door and you are told that in the hospital your third baby was mixed up with another one and you have the wrong child. How long after the switch happened would you swap the child you believed to be yours from birth so that you would have your biological child? (We are assuming in this dilemma that the other family will agree to whatever your decision is.)

Would you swap after 1 week?

Would you swap after 1 month?

Would you swap after 6 months?

Would you swap after 2 years?

Would you swap after 10 years?

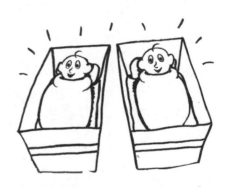

You'll be amazed how different people's answers are.

Two Brothers Dilemma

Two brothers were having a drink in a bar. One of the brothers got into an argument with the barman. The brother killed the barman despite the other brother attempting to stop the murder.

The judge had a decision to make. The brothers were conjoined twins. She wanted to convict the guilty man and send him to prison, but then the innocent brother would also go to prison.

Should she set them both free so a guilty man goes unpunished, or should she lock them both up so that an innocent man goes to prison?

Doctor Dilemma

You are a doctor with 3 adult patients all in need of an organ transplant. The first patient needs a kidney, the second a heart and the third a lung. They are all in critical condition.

You also have a fourth adult patient who has an incurable brain disease and will definitely die sometime in the next 48 hours. If he dies today, you will be able to save all 3 of the other patients with his organs. However, if he does not die until tomorrow, it will be too late and the other 3 patients will die.

You are in a remote hospital in very bad weather, so there is no chance of finding other donors in the next 24 hours. Would you help the fourth patient die peacefully so you can save the other 3, or would you allow him to die naturally and risk the other 3 passing away?

After you have discussed the dilemma, think about how you would feel if you knew the fourth patient.

THE BANDIT DILEMMA

You are transported back in time to the Wild West. You are the mayor of a small town of 100 people, all of whom know each other very well. A nasty group of bandits ride into town. They believe that someone in the town has told the local sheriff they robbed 3 banks. They call everyone into the square and say they will kill them all unless the person who told the sheriff comes forward.

Nobody steps forward as the bandits have confused your town with another one, and nobody has spoken to the sheriff. The bandits don't believe this, however. The head bandit gives you the gun and tells you to shoot 1 person or else he will shoot everybody in the town. Should you kill 1 person to save everyone else? If so, how would you decide who to kill?

CAR CRASH DILEMMA

You are in a 2-car crash in which you tragically hit a pedestrian and kill them. As you get out of the car, you see that the driver of the other car is crying as she believes she has killed the pedestrian. You know for sure that you are responsible, but would it ever make sense to allow the other driver to continue thinking that she hit the pedestrian? The other driver is 20 years older than you.

Birthday Paradox

You are in a room with a crowd of more than 30 people. Bet a friend that you think 2 people in the room have the same birthday. Most people will look around and take that bet thinking that there should be 183 (half a year of birthdays) people in a room before they would on average lose the bet.

Why should you be confident taking this bet?

This is an interesting statistic: once there are more than 21 people in a room there is a more than 50 per cent chance that 2 of them have the same birthday. You won't be right every time but you will be right more often than wrong. How do the statistics work? Ask your maths teacher!

A Sick Horse

In a farm stable there was a horse that was unable to stand and that looked very ill. The local vet confirmed that the horse was sick and delivered the news to the farmer. He said the horse would have to be put down if he did not improve in 3 days and he gave him some medicine.

A smart pig overheard the vet and he made the horse stand up and trot around the yard so that he would not be put down. It took a lot of hard work and effort but he eventually got the horse back on his feet.

After 3 days the farmer cried, "The medicine is working!" He was delighted and said, "We must have a big party. Let's kill the pig and have a feast!"

What is the moral of the story?

This can happen in life and in work. Often we don't see who is actually doing all the work and making things happen. Who does a lot of the work but maybe gets little praise? Maybe it's time you said thank you!

THE GENEROUS MILLIONAIRE

An Australian millionaire was on holiday with his family in the UK. After a busy day of hiking, they arrived very hungry in a village that had 2 pubs close to each other. They went to the first pub but were refused dinner as the time was 9.02 p.m. and the pub stopped serving at 9 p.m. exactly. The millionaire asked the owner if he would still serve him and his family as they were very hungry. The owner refused.

The millionaire and his family left and went to the second pub, which also stopped serving dinner at 9 p.m. However, the owner saw that the family were hungry and served them anyway, much to their delight.

When the millionaire was paying the bill of £22, he made the cheque out for £15,022. He said to the owner, "I will give you this cheque on 1 condition - that you show the cheque to the owner of the other bar."

What is the moral of the story?

THE MISSING DOLLAR

Three tourists go to a souvenir store after visiting the Empire State Building. They each buy a miniature Empire State for $10. The salesperson puts the money in the cash register. A few minutes after the tourists leave the salesperson realises that the miniature Empire States were on special offer: 3 for $25 instead of $30. She sends her assistant after the 3 tourists to give them back the extra $5.

When the assistant sees the tourists, he realises that he cannot split the money evenly between the 3 of them. As the tourists don't know what the special offer was, the assistant decides to give them $1 each and pocket the extra $2 as a tip.

Each tourist gets $1 back, so they each paid $9 for their miniature Empire State, totalling $27. The assistant kept the remaining $2.

But $27 + $2 = $29, and the tourists originally handed over $30. What happened to the missing dollar? Have a think before you read the answer.

BETTING SCAM

Henry received an email from an unknown source telling him the result of a football match that was being played later that day. This seemed unlikely to Henry, but it turned out that the prediction was correct

The next week, Henry received another email predicting the winner of another football match, and again the prediction was correct.

Over the next 5 weeks Henry received 5 more emails, all of which correctly predicted the result of a future football match. Then he received an email telling him that if he paid €500, he would receive 10 further correct predictions and therefore the ability to win a fortune. Henry thought about it and realised it was a scam. How did he realise this?

A Life Well Lived

The wisest people in life are often those who have lived the longest. There was a survey of people who were close to the end of their lives and it asked them what their biggest regrets were. Here were the top 5:

1. I wish I had not worked so hard and had played more.

2. I wish I had stayed in touch with my friends more than I did.

3. I wish I had let myself be happier.

4. I wish I had had the courage to be my true self and had followed my own dreams rather than doing what others expected of me.

5. I wish I had had the courage to express my feelings more.

Ask the adults around the table which of these they think they are not doing enough of right now.

CHAPTER 6

FAMILY FUN, FACTS and WORDS

Hilarious family games that you don't need a boardgame to play, fun facts and word challenges for all ages. Read on for great activities that can be done around a table with friends and family and games that can cause huge excitement and laughter.

CHINESE WHISPERS CHARADES

We've all heard of Chinese whispers and we've all heard of charades, but rarely a combination of both. Split the group in 2. One group leaves the room while the other group thinks of an activity. This can be something easy like "diving into a pool and swimming" or it can be difficult like "getting into your car and carefully reversing out of the driveway".

Once you have agreed your charade, invite the first person from the other team in and explain to them what they need to act out. Then the second person comes in from the team and the first person acts out the charade, with no talking. Then the third person comes in and the second person has to act out what they saw. This continues until the last person comes in and watches the second last person act out the charade. They then need to work out what it is that they are seeing. Rarely do they get it right!

What's hilarious is how much the charade will change each time. If they don't guess correctly, have the first person act it out again, this time for everyone, to see if that helps.

TOMMIE

Tommie is a high-stakes pressure game!

You take about 10 sweets and put them on a large table. One player leaves the room and those who are left choose a sweet that they will call "Tommie". The job of the player when they come back into the room is to *not* pick Tommie. Every time they pick a sweet that is not Tommie, they get to keep the sweet, but once they pick Tommie their turn is over. So if they pick Tommie first - no sweets for them! It's funny when their hand is hovering over a sweet and everyone else pretends that it is Tommie to try and trick them.

Everyone shouts "TOMMIE!" when a player picks that sweet.

HINT
You can play this with other age groups. Just change what you put in the middle. It does not have to be sweets.

REAL LIFE CLUEDO

This game is like Cluedo, but in real life. The objective is slightly different, though: you must "kill" all the other players and be the last person standing. The game works well over a weekend or on holidays, as it's not one you can play in an hour. Anyone from about age 7 to 97 can play!

First you will need 3 bowls.

Bowl 1: Take individual pieces of paper and write out what the main family areas are in the house. For example: kitchen, living room, hall, garden, etc. Do not use rooms where people are usually alone, such as the toilet or bedrooms. Put all the pieces of paper in the first bowl. There should be at least as many pieces of paper as there are players of the game.

Bowl 2: Have everyone write down a basic item from the house, for example, a spoon, a plate, a brush, a cup, a remote control, a candle, a newspaper, etc. They must be common items, so again don't choose an item like a toilet brush or a painting. Have everyone write their item on a piece of paper and put it into the second bowl.

Bowl 3: In the third bowl place everyone's names on separate pieces of paper.

Now everyone must take a piece of paper out of each of the 3 bowls. If you pick your own name, put it back in and choose again.

Everyone will now have a name, an item and a room, just like in Cluedo. For example: Clare, hall, remote control.

Your job now is to somehow hand the remote control to Clare in the hall. If you do this she dies and is knocked out! Once you achieve this you receive Clare's pieces of paper from the bowls. So she may have Kitty, kitchen, plate and then your job is to "kill" Kitty by giving her a plate in the kitchen.

The winner is the last person standing. You will be amazed how clever people are at getting people to take their item. Everyone starts off very suspicious so you need to be creative. The games work best over a day or a weekend because people can forget about it and then they get caught more easily.

BAD SINGING

This is really just a game to have fun at each other's expense. All you need is any device that allows you to listen to music on headphones. There are 2 ways to play.

The first is that you give a friend a song that only they can hear on the headphones. Their job is to sing the song using the same word over and over again - so "lah, lah, lah" or "doo, doo doo", etc.

It is up to everyone else to guess the tune. Sounds easy but people often aren't the best singers!

The second way to play is to give 1 person the headphones and turn the sound up high. The person has to sing the song that is playing. They must sing it with confidence, and the funny thing is that they cannot hear their voice but everyone else can. They'll be wondering why everyone is rolling around laughing. This works best when nobody in the group can sing! It can also help to give the singer the lyrics of the song if you like.

TRIBES

This is a game that works with between 9 and 14 players. Everyone takes a piece of paper, writes down a famous person and folds it up. This should be someone the group knows, and remember you may be playing with 8-year-olds and 80-year-olds, so they should be very well-known people. You can also choose to use names of people around the table, or names everyone is familiar with like a family pet name, as that can prove to be funny.

The list could be something like this:

Michelle Obama

Homer Simpson

Peter Cosgrove

Popeye

Spider–Man

Cristiano Ronaldo

Kim Kardashian

Will Smith

Grandma

Once all the names are written down, place them in a bowl. Get someone to read all the names out just once. You have to remember all the names but you cannot write them down. The names are then hidden from view.

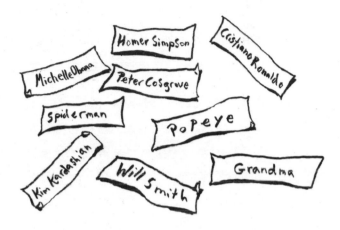

Start with the youngest person and get them to ask someone a simple question like "Are you Michelle Obama?" If the person says yes, they join the team (or tribe) of the person who guessed right. If the guess is incorrect then the person who was just asked gets to ask the next question. You keep going until a person or a tribe gets the last name. What is amazing is that as you near the end, people start forgetting what names have yet to be said.

It is best if you tell the players that they cannot mention the names during the game. So you cannot say "No one has said Homer Simpson in a while" as that helps people recall names they have forgotten.

HINT
For large groups sometimes you need to read the list of names out twice.

TRUE OR FALSE

Find out how fascinating our world and universe are while also quizzing your family on whether these facts are true or false.

1. The sun is 400 times the diameter of the moon, but by an amazing coincidence, it is also 400 times further from earth. This means that during an eclipse the sun appears the same size as the moon.

2. The sun is so big that you could fit 59 earths across the face of the sun.

3. There is a moon of Saturn that is shaped like a potato.

4. Stars in the universe can be bigger than the sun. The largest known star is VY Canis Majoris, whose diameter is 2 billion kilometres, which means it is 1,400 times bigger than the sun.

5. The heaviest known stuff in the universe is the matter in a neutron star. A sugar-cube-sized piece of neutron star would weigh the same as the weight of all humans in the world.

6. Krakatoa is the most powerful ever recorded volcano and in 1883 it erupted with the force of several nuclear bombs.

7. The Pacific Ocean contains more water than all the other seas put together.

8. The deepest point of the ocean is called Challenger Deep and it is 5,000 metres below sea level.

9. The coldest temperature ever recorded was -56.6°Celsius.

10. The longest single flight by a bird is made by the bar-tailed godwit, which has been tracked flying from Alaska to New Zealand without stopping - a distance of over 11,000 kilometres.

Word Funnage

» Two words in the English language begin with the letters *he* and finish with the letters *he*. What are they?

Answer: Headache and heartache.

» The only word in the English language to end *mt* is dreamt.

» Orange and purple have no words that rhyme with them - or so they say. But there is a word *sporange* and it is a very rare alternative form of the word sporangium, which means part of a fern. Hirple means to walk with a limp and rhymes with purple. So they do have words that rhyme!

» The word *queueing* is the only word with 5 consecutive vowels.

» If you like toilet humour, ask someone to say "Hoof-hearted. Ice melted." (Think about it!)

» There is no single-word name for the back of the knee. If you were in charge of making a word for it, what would it be?

» An ambigram is a word that looks the same from different viewpoints. For example, the word "SWIMS" will be the same even when turned upside down.

» The only 15-letter word that can be spelled without repeating a letter is *uncopyrightable*.

R WORDS

Ask a group around the table this question. Are there more words in the English language that begin with the letter r or words that have the letter r as their third letter?

ANSWER

If you were to bother to do the counting, you would discover that there are more words with r in the third position. However, most people say that there are more words with r in the first position because it is far easier to think of words that begin with r than it is to think of words that have r in the third position. After all, we do not tend to remember words according to what letter they have in the third position. So people come to the conclusion that there are more words that begin with r.

Thinking for Yourself?

We think that we always make up our own mind, but what we don't know is that people and companies are trying to make us think and act a certain way, especially when we are buying things. Try this trick on someone to demonstrate how easily we are influenced.

Write out the words below in capital letters and show them to a friend.

CLEAN

WASH

SO_P

Ask your friend to work out what the word with the missing letter is.

Now write out the 3 words below for another friend.

LUNCH
EAT
SO_P

Ask them to work out what the word with the missing letter is.

Your first friend will likely say "soap" and your second will likely say "soup". This is known as priming. The words in the first example relate to cleaning, so people immediately think of soap. In the second example the words relate to food, so people think of soup. It doesn't work every time but it works more often than not.

Indonesian Islands

Let's see how much free will we actually have when guessing an answer to how many islands there are in Indonesia. Most people have no idea how many islands there are. Split the group into 2 and separate the 2 groups so they can't hear each other.

To the first group, say:

You probably don't know the answer to this, but I want you to write down how many islands you think are in Indonesia. Don't give a round number like 150 or 180 or 200. I would prefer a number like 171 or 193.

To the second group, say:

You probably do not know the answer to this, but I want you to write down how many islands you think are in Indonesia. Please don't give me a round number like 25,000, or 30,000. I would prefer a number like 23,187 or 26,583.

There are actually 17,508 islands in Indonesia but the real trick here is to see if the first group give much lower answers than the second group because you primed them. By giving example answers like 150 and 200 you can often influence them without them knowing.

Lots of our decisions are not as independent as we like to think!

Three Word Games

These are fun word games to play as a group.

Game 1

Ask everyone to come up with the longest 1-syllable word they can. Give them 2 minutes. Tell them after a while that the longest word is 9 letters and there are more than 1. Then see how they do.

Possible answers: stretched, strengths, scratched, scrounged, scrunched, screeched.

Game 2

There is only 1 word that has 3 double letters beside each other. Some people like to think it is *woollen*, because if you spell it quickly - "double *u* double *o*, double *l*, *e*, *n*" - it sounds correct, but it isn't. This word starts with a *b*.

Answer: Bookkeeper

Game 3

Descenders are the parts of letters that descend below the line of the text like p, y or g and ascenders are the parts of letters that ascend above the main body of the letter, as in h, k and l.

Using only lower-case letters, see how long a word you can make without using any ascenders or descenders. For example, *cocoon* or *commissions*. But you can do much better than that! Rumour has it there are words up to 18 letters long.

Best (and almost impossible) answer: overnumerousnesses

Others good answers: curvaceousnesses, overnervousnesses, anniversaries

INTERESTING FACTS TO SHARE

» Until the late 1960s men with long hair were not allowed to enter Disneyland.

» By the age of 5, children have acquired 85 per cent of the language they will have as adults.

» Legend has it that if a statue of a person on a horse has both of the horse's front legs in the air, then the person died in battle. If the horse has 1 front foot in the air, the person died as a result of injuries received in battle. If the horse has all 4 legs on the ground then the person died of natural causes. Next time you go sightseeing check if this is true!

» Your brain uses up to 13 per cent less energy when you are watching TV than when you are doing nothing at all. This highlights the importance of us spending time away from all digital devices to get our brain to work!

» Paraguay is the only country in the world whose flag is different on both sides.

» More people are called Louis who live in St Louis, more dentists will be called Denise, and on average there are more

Georges in Georgia, Florences in Florida and Virgils in Virginia. I wonder what this says about the town "Fartrim" in Ireland?

» Frogs interpret food based on movement. Therefore if you put a frog in a box full of dead flies, it will starve to death as it won't be aware of any food. For a frog to recognise a dead fly as food you would have to lift up the dead fly and drop it down into the box. Then the frog would recognise it and grab it.

» 1961 was the last time the year read the same upside down as right side up. Any idea when the next will be? Answer: 6009.

» Two-thirds of the world's people have never seen snow.

» There are 100 billion galaxies in the world and we can only see 2,000 of them

» When you put a seashell to your ear, it's not the sea that you hear, it's blood flowing through your head.

» No matter how high or low an aeroplane flies, its shadow is always the same size.

» The buttons on a man's jacket sleeve were there originally to stop waiters from wiping their noses on the sleeves of their uniforms.

» The Romans had a room called a vomitorium for getting sick in. They loved their food so much they would often use a feather to tickle the inside of their throat to help them vomit so they could continue eating.

» The pupils of sheep's and goats' eyes are rectangular.

INTERESTING WORDS

Bumbershoot: this is another word for an umbrella and much more fun to say, e.g. "it's raining so please hand me my bumbershoot".

Zoantrophy: this is when people are mad and they think that they are an animal and not a person.

Snollygosters: these are people who cannot be trusted; let's be honest, how could you trust a snollygoster!

Tittle: this is the name of the dot that is over the i or the j.

Crapulence: this is an illness due to eating too much, often caused at the end of a 'trick or treating' sweet-eating session!

Acersecomic: a person who has never had a haircut.

Hallux: is the name for a person's big toe.

Lunule: is the name for the little half moons at the base of our fingernails and toenails.

Pandiculation: when you stretch out your body and arms when tired, usually accompanied with a yawn.

Lollygag: this is nothing to do with lollies; it means to be idle and lazy or to waste time. In the past you used to hear parents say to their kids "stop lollygagging".

Winklepicker: this is a style of shoes from the 1950s with a really pointy toe.

Caruncle: at the corner of your eye the little pink part is the caruncle.

Armstate: the hole in your jumper or shirt where you put your arm through.

Purlicue: the space between the extended thumb and index finger.

Jirble: means to spill a liquid while pouring it because your hands are shaking.

Blatherskite: a person who talks at great length without making much sense.

Hoddy noddy: this is another name to give a very foolish person or a simpleton.

Frankenfood: a recent word that denotes food that has been altered by science (e.g. genetically modified food). It comes from a mix of the words Frankenstein and food.

Tittynope: a small quantity of anything left over, like food you leave on your plate.

ANSWERS
CHAPTER 1: RIDDLES AND TEASERS

ANIMALS

1. Elephants cannot jump, so any animal that can jump even an inch can jump higher than an elephant can!

2. Easy! The other end of the rope is not tied to anything.

3. It's a centipede lying on its back with its 100 legs in the air!

4. One. After that the truck is no longer empty.

5. It is winter and the river is frozen over. The dog can walk across.

6. The mother's name was "What". There is no question mark at the end of the second sentence.

7. None. The rest get scared and fly away.

8. The thin cat is the fat cat's mother.

9. If 20 ate chickens then 10 did not.

WORDS

1. Inkstand - listen to it again. You will hear many people saying "kst, kst, kst".

2. Short. By adding "er" you get "shorter".

3. NOON.

4. The man wrote down "your exact weight" and won the bet.

5. Post office

6. "Nowhere" becomes "now here" when you add a single space.

7. Or.

8. Neither is correct. Tomatoes are a fruit!

9. "Are". Add an *a* to the end and you get "area".

NUMBERS

1. One. It only takes 1 brick to *complete* it.

2. The first number the teacher called out was zero. The answer had to be zero as any number multiplied by zero will be zero.

3. It has 2 syllables.

4. How long.

5. The answer is 3, not 2, as many think. Half of 2 is 1. Then add the 2 to make 3. You do the addition part second, not first.

6. I gave Anna the 2 marbles in the bag.

7. Forty.

8. 11 is the answer. The 10 extra from the 100 candles, and

then 1 more from burning the extra 10. Most people say 10 not 11!

DATES

1. The letter r.

2. All of them.

3. No time at all. The wall is already built.

4. Yesterday, today and tomorrow.

5. Jane's birthday is on December 31, when she turned 19. If we say this on January 1 (which it must be) then she was 18 the day before yesterday. She will turn 20 at the end of this year, and 21 next year. (This one is very confusing!)

6. There is no 31 September. (The other parts of the riddle are just there to confuse you!)

7. He was born in 1860 BC, so the year decreases as his age increases.

GAMES

1. Playing chess with Eugene.

2. In the third sentence "it" refers to the piece that was cut off, not the stick.

3. He throws it in the air.

4. Prison.

5. A tissue.

6. Your left hand (or your left elbow).

7. He lives in Alaska, where the sun rises only once every 6 months.

8. Ann is blind and she reads Braille.

TRAVEL

1. Alice is in first class in school, not on the plane!

2. All of the men were married. None of them were *single*, so every *married* man was wet.

3. People don't knock on their own hotel room door.

4. He used 1 wheel nut from each of the other 3 wheels.

5. The accountant and the lawyer were women, so John must have been the doctor.

6. Because Mr Blyth was snoring.

7. An anchor.

8. The helicopter is on a launchpad on top of a skyscraper, 300 metres above the ground.

9. They will be the same distance away because they will be right beside each other!

MISCELLANEOUS

1. A saw, a hairdryer and a telescope. I didn't say you had to

use the same thing to do all 3!

2. "You will shoot me." They cannot shoot him as then he would be telling the truth and they cannot hang him as he will be lying if they hang him. So he has found a way out!

3. An apple a day keeps the doctor away, which was what he wanted to do.

4. Emily, of course.

5. Harrison is a priest.

6. He was cleaning the windows inside the building.

7. Because a round manhole cover cannot fall down the hole.

8. Her home is a bungalow.

9. A plant.

CHAPTER 2: TRICKS OF THE MIND

PUZZLE 1: THE ROPE BRIDGE

The interesting part to this puzzle is many do not think to send the 2 slowest people together. So send across the 1- and 2-minute people first and the 1-minute person can return with the torch.

Then send the 5- and 10-minute people across.

Then the 2-minute person can return with the torch.

Then the 1- and 2-minute people cross together and you have done it in 17 minutes and escaped the rabid wolves.

PUZZLE 2: CHICKEN AND FOX

Take the chicken over to the other side. Go back and take the grain over next, but instead of leaving the chicken with the grain, take the chicken back in the boat. When you reach the side with the fox, leave the chicken on the first side and take the fox back with you this time. Leave the fox on the side with the grain. Finally, go back over and get the chicken and take it over.

PUZZLE 3: LIFT PROBLEM

The man is very short and the buttons are quite high on the wall with the larger numbers higher up on the wall. The highest number he can reach on the elevator buttons is 11, except if it's raining, when he is able to use his umbrella to reach the button for the sixteenth floor.

PUZZLE 4: FIVE QUESTIONS

You can obviously use whatever questions you want for the first 3. It's all about distracting them with question 4 so they are caught off guard by question 5.

PUZZLE 5: ALL THE NUMBERS

$$^{35}/_{70} + {}^{148}/_{296} = 1$$

PUZZLE 6: 2 DOORS, 1 QUESTION

Ask this question to either guard: "What door would the other guard tell me to choose?" then choose the opposite door. Think about it! Both guards will point to the wrong door if you ask that question.

PUZZLE 7: THE 5 HATS

Black. Here's how he knew:

Start with the first student to respond. He's sitting in the back of the line where he can see the 2 students in front of him, and he doesn't know what colour hat he has on. There are 3 black hats and only 2 white hats, so if he had seen white hats on both of the students in front of him, he would have known that he had a black hat on. Therefore, we know that he does not see 2 white hats in front of him. The fact that the first student couldn't solve the riddle tells the student in the middle of the line something important: he and the student in front of him cannot both be wearing white hats. That leaves 3 options.

1.) Both he (the student in the middle) and the student in front are wearing black hats.

2.) The student in front is wearing a white hat, while he (the student in the middle) is wearing a black one.

3.) The student in front is wearing a black hat, while he (the student in the middle) is wearing a white one.

If the student in the middle had seen the man in front wearing a white hat, he would have known that option 2.) is the correct one and that he himself was wearing a black hat. Because he didn't figure out what colour hat he has on, we know that he must see a black hat in front of him, as that would leave open the possibility that he was wearing either colour.

Now consider the 3 choices from the perspective of the student in the front. He doesn't know which of the remaining choices, 1) or 3), is the correct one. But in either scenario, he must be wearing a black hat. So after thinking logically he gets it right and gets an A for logic!

PUZZLE 8: FUNNY MATHS

What you generally find is that even though the equations obviously give you the same answer - which for the record is: 40,320 - when someone sees the big number at the start they generally will estimate a much higher number than the person who sees the small number at the start.

PUZZLE 9: CARD TURN

The answer is "A and 7" but almost everyone says "A and 2".

A - is obvious; you need to turn this card to check there is an even number on the other side, so almost everyone gets this right.

K - there is clearly no need to do anything here as it's not a vowel so it is irrelevant.

2 - this is the one people say, but it is incorrect. The rule is that if there is a vowel on one side there is an even number on the other BUT not, if there is an even number on one side there has to be a vowel on the other side.

7 - this is the one people don't think about. What if there is a vowel on the other side? You need to check because if there is a vowel on the other side then not every card with a vowel has an even number on the other side.

Almost everyone will be scratching their head with this one!

PUZZLE 10: CARD DISTRACTION

You start dealing from the bottom of the deck, giving yourself the first card and then going around in an anti-clockwise direction.

PUZZLE 11: A FUNNY EQUATION

Turn the page upside down.

PUZZLE 12: COINS ON A TABLE

Harry puts the 5-cent piece on the floor under the table. This means he is also putting it under the 10-cent piece!

PUZZLE 13: TWO BIBLES

He owned both of the Bibles. Now the remaining one would be worth €10 million.

PUZZLE 15: EYES OPEN

There are two "the"s in the first sentence. Many people only look at the diagram and miss this error

PUZZLE 16: GHOST WORD

Ghoti is a constructed word to illustrate how weird English spelling is. Ghoti is pronounced fish. Yes, fish!

The *gh* is pronounced as in the word "tough".

The *o* is pronounced as in the word "women".

The *ti* is pronounced as in the word in "nation".

Put these together and you get fish. The word is known as a ghost word.

PUZZLE 17: 12 ORANGES

Squeeze the oranges and then give everybody the same amount of juice in a glass.

PUZZLE 18: WORD SHRINK

Startling, starting, staring, string, sting, sing, sin, in, I.

PUZZLE 19: A THOUSAND EIGHTS

$888 + 88 + 8 + 8 + 8 = 1,000$. You may find other, more complicated, answers also.

PUZZLE 20: THE MISSING LETTER

Like everything when you know the answer it looks easy, but because they have just heard the word "many" they will run through the alphabet and you will hear them saying "benny, cenny, denny, fenny" until they realise the correct word is "deny", which does not sound like "many". Some will get it quickly but you will be surprised how many are stumped for a long time.

PUZZLE 21: FIND THE ERRORS

"Are" is used twice instead of once.

"Misteak" is not a word. It should be "mistake".

The word "to" is repeated (although it is harder to spot than the two "are"s)

There is no full stop.

However, that is only 4. The fifth mistake is that there are only 4, not 5, mistakes!

PUZZLE 22: 15 MINUTES

» Start both simultaneously.

» When the 7-minute hourglass runs out, that is the moment when you start to measure the target 15 minutes.

» Four minutes after the 7-minute hourglass runs out, the 11-minute hourglass will run out (that's the first 4 minutes).

» Flip the 11-minute hourglass over immediately to measure another 11 minutes, bringing the time to exactly 15 minutes.

PUZZLE 23: OPTIMIST OR PESSIMIST?

You will be amazed how many more people choose the pessimistic:

"opportunity is nowhere" as opposed to the optimistic "opportunity is now here".

PUZZLE 24: TWO HORSES

Ride the other son's horse!

PUZZLE 25: RACE CAR TIME

Although the drivers could not use any clocks or watches, as they drove the same car they were able to use something. The first driver started the course and immediately turned on the wipers. He concentrated on how many times the wipers swiped and he then told the second driver to aim for the same number of wiper swipes.

PUZZLE 26: MYSTERY HOUR

Every year, we put the clocks forward an hour on the final Sunday of March. At 1 a.m. everyone puts their clocks forward to 2 a.m., so technically that hour does not exist and nothing can happen.

PUZZLE 27: UNIQUE WORDS

Take the first letter and move it to the end of the word and it spells out the word backwards! Amazing!

PUZZLE 28: STRANGER DANGER

The poison was in the ice, not in the lemonade, so because Lucy drank her drink quickly, the ice had yet to melt and there was less poison in her lemonade.

Chapter 5: Ways to be the Centre of Attention

FAMOUS INTERVIEW QUESTION

Give the car keys to your old friend and let them take the old woman to the hospital. Then stay behind and wait for the bus with the partner of your dreams.

MISSING DOLLAR

This is one that can be very hard to explain. So get someone who feels they understand to try and watch them get confused! The correct way to add up the total is to look at where all the money actually is. There is $25 in the cash register, $2 in the assistant's pocket, and each of the 3 tourists has $1. So there is nothing missing.

Confused? So is everyone!

BETTING SCAM

Henry was right - it was a scam. The predictions are correct because the scammer is predicting every result and he sends out emails to a huge number of people.

It goes like this:

The result will always be a win, lose or draw - 1 of 3 possible results.

If the scammer writes 3 emails - one predicting a win, one predicting a draw and one predicting a loss - and sends them out to 1 million people, 333,333 people will get an email that correctly predicts the winner.

The scammer does the same a second time, but this time just to the 333,333 people who got the correct email the first time. This time, on average 111,111 people will get the correct result.

The scammer then sends a third round of emails to the 111,111 people from the second group, and approximately 37,000 of the 111,111 people will receive the correct prediction a third time in a row.

The scammer can do this 7 times and there will still be around 2,312 people who have received 7 emails predicting the correct result every time, so by that stage of course they will think they are on to a winner . . . but they aren't!

CHAPTER 6: FAMILY FUN, FACTS AND WORDS

TRUE OR FALSE

1. True.

2. False. You could actually fit 109 earths across the diameter.

3. True. Usually moons are relatively spherical because

gravity pulls the material into a sphere or ball shape, but this moon, called Hyperion, does not have enough gravity and is therefore shaped more like a potato.

4. True. VY Canis Majoris is a red hypergiant star almost 4,000 light years away and it is 1,400 times bigger than our sun.

5. True. A neutron star is the core of a giant star that has collapsed. It does seem a crazy thought that a sugar cube could weigh up to a billion tonnes!

6. True. It was 4 times more powerful than the largest nuclear bomb ever detonated.

7. True.

8. False. Challenger Deep is the deepest point but it is actually nearly 11,000 metres below sea level.

9. False. The coldest temperature ever recorded was in Antarctica and it was -89.2 degrees Celsius in 1983. 56.6 degrees Celsius was actually the hottest temperature ever recorded in Death Valley California in 1913.

10. True. It can fly further without stopping than almost any airplane.

If you enjoyed *Family Fun Unplugged* you can continue to bend your brain, fool your family and fascinate your friends with ...

Fun Unplugged is packed with puzzles, brainteasers and riddles that will have you and your friends scratching your heads for hours on end.

These code-breaking, fortune-telling tricks of the mind, and much more, will help you to surprise, astonish and befuddle everyone around you.

Fun Unplugged is guaranteed to give you endless entertainment and to impress any audience!